THE KEYS

Anna Billings-Vice

Scribe of Christ

"There is no more perfect beauty than what is given us from Our Father within."

-Father-

The Twelve Scribes of the Truth of Love

Mary Rydman

Rev. Pamela Whitman
Lee Flynn
Rev. Carl Lammers
Micah Sanger
Rev. Reja Joy
Sam Kirschner
Rev. Harrison Blackmond
Chris Souchack
( ) Bryce Boyd
Paula Benanti
Francis Hofmann

On July 5th, 2017, I was given the list of above names from Jesus. He called them "The Twelve Chosen Scribes. I was directed to give them no instructions. I was to simply give this work to them and they will know what to do with it. And, it will bring them great joy. This above list also contains the names of my greatest teachers of A Course in Miracles, which changed my life forever. They helped set me free and for this I am eternally grateful. Who are your Twelve? Who are your greatest Teachers?

THE KEYS

CHAPTER ONE: The Garden

CHAPTER TWO: The Betrayal

CHAPTER THREE: The Crucifiction

Chapter Three (Cont.)

CONTENTS

CHAPTER ONE

The Garden

If you find yourself here, I will join with you to show you the way out. I will point to the path we will take together. – Father -

The Body is a Wholly Neutral

"We are that awareness which the Creator extended. We are finally learning how to surrender. Don't stop asking, 'what would you have me do now'? Take it easy on yourself. I am going to continue to practice surrender and focus on true awareness." Rev. Carl ACIM OE CC 2017

Child of the Light, there is no difference between one form and another. Source of thought and perception are integral parts of one another. God in His great mercy provides a way out of misguided perceptions through the Holy Mind. The Holy Mind contains all minds with a joined purpose. It is not a wonder more people do not understand how to connect to their purpose? The Holy mind is the Source of Love. The Holy Mind only exist within you. It is the center of all Love. If you are not connected to your Holy mind, you cannot be consciously connected to the Holy Mind in another. At any given time, they too, are not connected to their Holy Mind and therefore not consciously to yours. This is where everything goes amiss. You see each other just as bodies. -Father-

The body is a neutral tool, including all the senses. Let go of right and wrong. Ask for the At-One-Ment. Ask, and ye shall receive the end of the divided mind. When this is accomplished you will see us as indistinguishably one. All thoughts of like purpose flow across the spectrum. Align the will, align the purpose, then all perceptions change. -Father-

Refuse to allow certain thought trains and the tracks will no longer be laid. You cannot free yourself from your ego. Only I can do that. Stop accepting your own analysis of the situation. Silently, listen to the whisper. It is not driven like the ego thought system. It does not manipulate the emotions. Within it, is Peace recognized. Knowledge is gently received. Revelation is the new way of understanding. Gone, is the self-motivated healing. -Father-

If you determine the path to healing, I cannot help you find resolution. You must let go of it. Let your mind be emptied, so it can be filled with Holy thoughts. The ego does not understand itself. It is like a small child playing in a field of tall grass. The only way out, is back through the trail already created. With the ego, it seems you must move backward to move forward. The Holy Spirit transcends the field and can see all the paths leading to the misfortune. It clearly sees the way in, is not the way out. The ego will only lead you back to where you were before. Freedom does not lie in the past and previous, ego methods of what you see as resolution. -Father-

The Revelation

"You are the Light at the center of my life." Mary ACIM OE CC 2017

This is what I am here for. The illusion is like a wasteland. You can find the echoes of heaven through your brothers and sisters who choose to serve their function. God is good, though few know it here. It is alright to cry while you still see it, for life without its Source clearly intact is utter chaos. Do not be ashamed when you stumble. It is nothing, really. It is hard to look upon hell and not cry but remember they do not understand yet. They think they fight alone against insurmountable odds. They do not know I will walk beside them and will show them the way out. -Father-

Be a beacon of Light to them. Therefore, you must forgive them their dark illusions. Pray with Love for them their nightmares will end soon. Believe not in their illusions for then you dream with them. Walk in Peace so they can see it is possible. -Father-

The Self-Alone
"Do not strain or make undo effort." Sam ACIM OE CC 2017

The self-alone is the belief you are alone in changing your mind. The choice is all that is needed. The Holy Spirit is within. The answer is always Love. There is only abundance. Remember, forward is better than backward, because you will actually get somewhere. – Father -

"Contemplation opens my heart." Rev. Regina Dawn Akers, The Teachings of the Inner Ramana

The Repurposing of the Body
"Love created me like itself." Rev. Pam ACIM CC Lesson 67

You cannot escape illusions without the body at this point

3

because you still believe in death. The amount of suicide in your world states this concept clearly. Misunderstanding the purpose of the body is critical to the ego structure. If you are anxious to let it go, maybe you have misunderstood its purpose. Is it possible, the way out of illusions is in correcting this misperception? Is it possible, death flips the coin, but the illusions remain to dim the perception of the Light within? If you cannot see the Light within while in form, understand its presence can still evade you in death. This is demonstrated in the existence of the dark, near, death experience. Their concepts of fear, guilt and sin follow them even once the body illusion is dropped. Because it is Love that is being avoided while imprisoned in the body, the Soul must recognize it has been using the body to hide from Love. -Father-

One will not suddenly drop resistance even when shown Love and offered its eternal blessing. Thus, you come back to bodies and misuse them, missing the mark in the dark: a prison with five recognized senses. You, who recognize your connection with the Holy Mind are either seen as exceptional or crazy. I assure you, "crazy" is of the ego. A split mind cannot recognize its own division. Do not place your allegiance in division. Down and out, it is through your illusions you avoid Love, and divide yourselves over and over. -Father-

"There is nothing outside of God." Chris ACIM OE CC 2017

The Deep State of Separation
"I am, that which I seek." Bryce ACIM OE CC 2016

A man who sees himself as a purely physical being, and only that, only sees a physical world. He avoids the recurring question of "why am I here?", because the answer is glum: Live for an undetermined amount of time and it is "over", and "time is short". Indeed, there is never enough time. How could there be? How can anyone feel hope? The ego's version of the world is hopeless and hapless.

The uncertain purpose of life causes immense distress in the minds of men. There are two worlds as a result of the split mind: the egoic world and the real world. One world cannot be viewed through the other world's lens. Only the Holy Spirit within can provide the lens for proper viewing. It is the discovery of this viewing lens within that ultimately leads to the process of regeneration. At first, you get mere glimpses through the inner lens. As you settle into your being through your willingness to provides moments of stillness, you will find the glimpses through the lens are tolerated longer and become more and more enjoyable. Removing stubborn filters, is tedious, but necessary. It is your view that needs to change, not the view itself. -Father-

"Love created me like itself." Rev. Pam ACIM CC Lesson 67

We seek for Love in so many forms, not seeing the first form has all that is needed to hide from Love or find Love depending on which view you choose to see through. God bless those who can see through the proper lens. -Father-

"Holiness created me Holy. Kindness created me kind. Helpfulness created me helpful. Perfection created me perfect." Rev. Pam ACIM CC Lesson 67

When the transformation is complete, you will have transcended death, not because you seek to be eternal, but because you have chosen for Love and now you are no longer stuck terrified, wishing to destroy yourselves. -Father –

"This Light was everywhere and everything. The Light was projecting the body into this dimension. The body was like a hologram, but it was energetic." Micah ACIM OE CC 2017

Look for the Changeless

"Look at the formless... those things of and in creation that do not change." Micah ACIM OE CC 2017

The grapes of wrath will be crushed under the feet of forgiveness and be made into wine, flooding all the world in Love. The thief, the saint and the murderer were made one through forgiveness. You are literally choosing which reality you support. The energy/frequency multiplies through the support of the ego's illusion of reality. If you support war, you see war. Cease to believe in death and its resultant ideas and it will disappear from your consciousness. I do not need your help, just your willingness. You must learn to accept what is and what has always been so. All life must be respected, for all life comes from the same Source. Energy sent out is returned to its source. Do not speak of illusions of the past you no longer want to make real. God is not in illusions and neither is your identity. You can simply let go of what you no longer want. -Father-

"The Holy Spirit is there waiting for my recognition." Sondra ACIM OE CC 2017

Creating is never a waste of time. Let me, free you from the fear of doing what you Love. It is about time, we find each other among the chaos. Let us formulate a plan for a loving answer. God has no idea of the contrary ideas of the ego because they are not true creations. Projections of the creative heart into the hologram are the real content of God, the central Source of all life. Disordered thinking is simply reabsorbed into the wholeness. Do not be afraid to let go of what does not have to exist for you. Disrupted thought is only a lack of concentration. Distraction is of the ego. Ask the Holy Spirit to subjugate the recycling mind. -Father-

"My mind is attracted to what I like. So, my focus increases and my ego is fixated on my need. The ego's only real purpose in my mind is to deny me peace through beliefs of imposition. So, then I judge them. Let me forgive those impositions." Bryce ACIM OE CC 2017

The Two Rabbits

Jesus said, "Know what is within your sight, and what is hidden from you will become clear to you. For there is nothing hidden that will not be revealed." Secret Teachings of Jesus, The Gospel of Thomas, Saying 5

Do you know what happens when a man tries to catch two rabbits? If he is lucky, he catches the weaker one. Choose for the stronger rabbit, the single One and I assure you a confident gain. Don't struggle against the self and chase the weaker rabbit. There is truly, no gain whatsoever. What has been taught, continues to be taught to the masses. What is fed to the masses, as babes in the cradle grows to maturity then fades back into the aqueous, whether recognized or not. Let it fade. Teach the babes a new way. One, times one always equals one whether recognized or not. - Father -

Children emanate the original, conjugal joining that produced the innocent Christ. The Christ flows and rest in their wide, innocent eyes and small, new bodies. In their innocence, they do not pretend to know what the body is for. Its function is still clearly intact. The extension, the powerful drive to be joyful and happy, is the direct experience of the Christ within. Children are therefore always fulfilling their function. -Father-

"Your practice rests on your willingness to let all littleness go. Finally, you will learn there is no limit to where you are." Micah

The World Within

There is reward for consistently seeking the Kingdom within. You first must recognize there is something inside you, which you do not yet understand. Once you do begin to look within, you will come to see there is nothing to fear. You are not alone in the endeavor to find happiness and Peace within yourself despite the exterior circumstances.

There is an undisturbed, unchanging Source to tap, but you cannot find what you do not seek. I am not saying it is easy to believe or grasp as of yet, but you will find it a worthwhile endeavor. The split mind has no desire to heal, for it does not see there is a problem. Remember, you cannot chase two rabbits and hope to catch either one. The portal is more open or less open in direct proportion to the blocks to Love's presence, as Heaven exists within a pure state of Love. – Father -

"I am as God created me." Rev. Pam ACIM CC Lesson 94

Because Love is so, it still does not stand recognized as the constant that holds all together. Man, still sees himself through separate identities. So, they combine their egos, mimicking the constant and create a world of intermittent chaos, as it adds (joins) or subtracts (separates) from itself. As man adds or subtracts, he is either at odds or stands even with his brother. Stop focusing on bodies and bodies seeking each other, and bodies will cease to be the focus. Let us go into the house of Love. There really is no other way to cleanse the cup. -Father-

"The most important person to be honest with is myself." Aida ACIM OE CC 2017

The constant only knows one solution, Love. Any words are literally nothing if not shared. So, the ego mind shares its chaos even though it seeks autonomy. The return to comfortable numbness is indeed a choice, but no choice of the ego is real. Therefore, chaos is always a temporary condition. A single mind cannot express a true singularity without being multiplied by one, thus joining and becoming truly one. The singularity cannot be altered through division. One divided by one, remains ne, but the apparent oneness is not always apparent. -Father-

"Only the past can separate, and it is nowhere." Micah ACIM OE CC 2017

When temptation comes, look within. Silence the mind by not holding onto specific thought forms. Do not try to create a way out for yourself. You cannot see Love's presence from the doorway you stand in. Enter the place you no longer wish to occupy. Is it not crazy to be afraid of Love? Yet, you are still standing in the doorway looking in. You are offering no true commitment to yourself. Yes, the view is nice, but you remain unchallenged. The heart mending remains out of your reach through your refusal to walk through the doorway and demonstrate Love's Truths to those you hold dearest.

The doorway to Love's presence has always remained open. You see it is open and yet you refuse to engage your relationships and let Love flow. In Truth, you fear its depth. You fear it will swallow you up, but you must try. Truly, put one foot in front of the other, take baby steps. I will engage you fully. Together we must deal with the demons that continue to haunt you. -Father-

"I will accept my part in God's plan for salvation." Rev. Pam ACIM CC Lesson 145

The Lamb of God cannot be found in or through a harden heart. We must soften you. This you fear. The abyss cannot swallow you. Lack of Love is not real. We, together, can refine your heart and bring you Peace. You have been having glimpses of this healing. The visions of your Father here on Earth are, but mere glimpses of Him in heaven. You have hidden yourself from the Truth. The most loving answer has always been there for you to choose for. Sometimes, the most obvious answer is the right one. Don't choose for disaster by not paying attention to your heart. -Father-

"It is quiet, It is silent, It is at rest, and It is before everything." The Secret Teachings of Jesus, Book of Thomas

In answer to attack, stay in the good and pray. Energy sent out is returned to its source. Be the guardian of your thought system. Supported frequency eventually produces form. So, look for the recycling thoughts. – Father –

Visiting the Miracle Principles

"God's peace and joy are mine. Today, I will accept God's peace and joy (which are mine), in glad exchange for all the substitutes which I have made for happiness and peace. Let me be still and listen the truth." Rev. Pam ACIM CC Lesson 11

Are you ready for the interconnectedness of feeling whole once again? You are a Son of God when you recognize the world within. There is no god you want in ego illusions. You choose each moment which lens to view from. Within, there is a lens that will correct your sight. It is not up to you to make this lens. Throw away the old mechanisms of thought. You will know which lens you have chosen by concepts of separation. Do you feel connected or disconnected to your brothers and sisters? All the senses will become one, once again. Remember, the separation created all separate experiences. -Father-

"I am embracing my humanness. I am embracing myself, my big self, my little self." Paula ACIM OE CC 2017

The Cave Analogy

"My adjustors are still in Israel." Rhett ACIM OE CC 2017

It is as if you are sitting in a cave and you have chosen the darkest corner. You are hungry and frightened. You pray for help because you cannot see and do not know the way out. At the time of physical birth, in your descent into form, it took a considerable amount of time to adjust to the new paradigm. It was a new kind of light and a new kind of necessary air. At first, you can barely see, and this new air burns your unused lungs. I assure you, returning Home and leaving the physical is a much easier than this, but it takes your trust and willingness.

Unlike the ego's version of reality, it will not be thrust upon you. It is wonderful and joyous to return Home. It is exactly the opposite to the ego's version of being born. Birth, to the ego is a painful, separation process. Birth of the Soul is pure Joy. The ego's interpretation of all things must eventually be let go of. It is inherent in the reversal of thought processes that there be some confusion. Each step inward is a step toward the awareness of heaven here in this moment. -Father-

"Fear is a symptom of your deep sense of loss." Lee ACIM OE CC

So, dear, Holy Child, I stand at the cave's entrance peering in at you. Can you see me here? Look again. I am here within the Light. Can you feel the warmth of Light and Love being extended to you from creation? I have sat in this very cave. I have sat on that very bench holding my face in tear-drenched hands. Do you really understand I have walked the world? That I, along with you have been afraid to come out of the cave? Do not despair for you are not alone. It is an illusion child. So, we shall start here, my Love. Please, remove your wet hands from your tear, strained eyes and look at what I have laid at your feet. It is a lamp and it is mine. -Father-

"The Holy Spirit replaces fear with Love." Lee ACIM OE CC

The Empowerment of God
"There is no loss in the Will of God." Rev. Pam ACIM CC

Not all of humanity can experience Love. We all can remember a time of having a hardened heart. It is not that you are extending Love improperly when it is not recognized, it is to whom you are extending it that is producing the experience. Not all Love is recognized as such and therefore rejected. Extend it anyway. Remember, when you send Love to one, you send Love to all. Just as you put up barricades to your brother's expressions of Love so does your brother put up blocks to your expressions of Love. -Father-

An animal will not attack you unless you are afraid. It is the fear that sets up the attack. Why? Because fear is lack of Love. Man projects fear because he, himself is a fear-filled being. Man is fearful of the retribution and intensity of the rage and fear he, himself projects outward, for it is returned in like kind. Enjoy yourself today. Your process is set. You do not need to struggle for freedom. -Father-

"No one can fail who asks to reach the truth." Rev. Pam ACIM CC 131

The Light is in the Tunnel

"We are all travelers in this world. From the sweet grass to the packing house, birth til' death, we travel between the eternities." Broken Trail

God is in a format you do not yet fully understand. Once you do you will be free of the ideology your Spirit can be identified from its container. Do not fill yourself with preconceived ideas, for they will fool you into thinking you have helped yourself. As I said before, resign as your own teacher for the Holy Spirit cannot be fooled by your ego, but you can. -Father-

"Shift from the dream of isolation." Micah ACIM OE CC 2017

You must go through it not around it. Only Love, can lead you out of your nightmares. God is not in them. You are mistaking the landscape of God as the world you created. Within the landscape, you are creating a nightmare of your own egoic choosing. Drop the nightmare and notice the majesty of the landscape of loving thoughts reflected all around you. God is in the changeless. Your world shifts from day to night as a reflection of an inner Truth. Such as, you cannot see in the night without a light source. This is reflected to you from an inner Truth: You cannot see without your Source. If creation were a reflection of your egoic state, you would be in a constantly shifting, spatial world. But God, Our Source, is constant. So, physical laws remain constant despite your shifting egoic perceptions. Man's, egoic mind cannot make true constants of any kind. Only the mind of God is stable, therefore stability can only be from its Source. -Father-

"Everything is a manifestation of Divinity." Rev. Pam ACIM CC

Man would like to shift the focus to the created order of things and say "this" or "that" is what needs to be left behind. It is the world of your egoic creation you need leave behind. Through your willingness you will be set free from your illusions of what you think is real and unreal. There is no meaning to the concept of letting go of mountains, trees and rocks. This is not the part of the world you need to let go of. Rarely, do you attack a rock or fear attack from a rock. Indeed, this has no meaning. So, while you may put concerted effort into letting go of the fishes and birds, you have spent no time trying to let go of the blocks to Love's presence within.

Often, men set forth to fight with each other over truly meaningless concepts instead of looking for the solution for Love's absence between them. This is wholly true of war. From the smaller scales of attack concepts to the larger, it is all the same. Man is avoiding Love. So, the wars continue great and small until a chosen awakening among enough Souls occurs. -Father-

"No matter how great the message, it cannot be heard if it is not shared." Katherine ACIM OE CC 2017

The Physical Principle
"I will not value, the valueless" Rev. Pam ACIM CC

You can blow up a mountain with a bomb, but you cannot change the physical constants that created the mountain, nor what blew it up. All gets reorganized and regenerated in the physical realm, and this too, is a reflection of the spiritual state of man. Look again, at all the unchanging constants before you. This is God. This is heaven because of the projection of constancies that can only come from Our Source. So, I say again, heaven has been here all along. It is man's mind that is absent. If you did not believe you were a body, the created order of things would not disturb you so.

You would see it as what it is, a reflection of Divine Love and Truth and you would sing praises. How can one not jump for

Joy when a super nova is seen as a reflection of a Soul bursting forth with Love? Perspective is skewed by your belief in smallness. When you begin to wake and see, you are a part of the God that spewed forth this magnificence, you will surely be seen a super nova. You will be so in Love with the All of creation, your Love will dance across the skies of this Heaven. -Father-

And Jesus said, "You know that the spiritual and material is merged within the Christ." Secret Teachings of Jesus, Book of James

Undefended

"If I defend myself, I am attacked. But, in defenselessness, I will be strong, and I will learn what my defenses hide." Rev. Pam ACIM CC Lesson 135

You can fast forward through time and illusions if you so choose. But, it may come to pass, you will find you would like to revisit some of your cherished dreams of Love. You see, in your determination to see past time and end your illusions of having a body, you will find still nothing there. Let us go back and look at time's content. What did you go there seeking? Oh yes... Love and yet, you find nothing. You will not find revelation in time's second, but in God's moment which is everlasting, transcending time's endless march. The ticking clock remains motionless when seen from the inside out. -Father-

"Into His presence would I enter now." Rev. Pam ACIM CC Lesson 157

The crucifixion was not my greatest, spiritual challenge. It was the everyday living and the human interactions that presented my greatest challenges. I was not here to die. I was here to show others how to truly live. Only the world, would see death as the ultimate battle, for this is its focus. Man does not walk alone for a reason. He would have no reflective base from which to learn. A divided mind cannot heal itself, for it cannot see the division. As you look upon the division in your brother's mind, you look upon your own. -Father-

"Forgiveness is the willingness to let go of hurt." Wendy ACIM OE CC 2017

God has blessed you and you have come to see me still there with you. I never left my place beside you. You are my care-takers in the world of form. I await your waking moments to give you guidance. I am. The small, soft voice is mine. I am not a divider. You cannot add more substance to an already overflowing chalice. Man must recognize his mind is full and empty it through his willingness to go within and find him-self. Revelation is given you. When he arrives, he becomes aware of how full his mind is of worldly thoughts and con-cerns. Give this world over to me for a moment. -Father-

"For He Loves what he sees within you, and He would extend it." Lee ACIM OE CC

The Scribe of Christ
"Today I learn to give as I receive." Rev. Pam ACIM CC Lesson 158

Hold fast to the thoughts I place in you this day. For, I have no agenda that will harm. All thoughts from me are pure and free of judgement. You are beauty. You are Love: a gentle flower that does not question its existence or how it will be sus-tained. I have so many, beautiful surprises to share with you. Let our beauty shine forth from your eyes as you look upon the master illusion. For, as your sight opens suddenly you will see my holiness shining forth from what you once saw as darkness. We are One. We are Holy. I am the water you drink.

You are no longer apart from me. I am the solution to the unsolved. I am the Here and Now. I am the Holy Light from which All have come. Be peaceful and learn from me. You are whole and perfect. There is no struggle to have me with you. This is an illusion the ego would have you hold onto to maintain separation from me. Rejoice, for I am here. – Father -

There are no errors the Holy Spirit cannot correct. Your interactions with your brothers are leading you both Home. The ego will offer up a myriad of solutions to correct for your perceived errors. It always seeks to make one "right" and one "wrong": one Holy, the other vilified. Our Father has no desire to condemn His creation. There is not one among you who can stand as judge and jury for what you do not understand. This is why I ask you to look with me upon all relationships you choose to enter. You are both groping in the dark, trying to find each other in limited forms of what you both believe you are.

I am only there in your awareness if you invite me in. The Holy Spirit has written my memory upon your hearts. Listen carefully when you pray, for The Scribe of Christ is joyfully sharing with you what was written in your heart eons ago, but which you are having difficulty remembering. The Scribe of Christ was placed there for you, dear One. As the ancient Truths enter your memory once again, the Holy in the heavenly realms leap for Joy. The Love in them sing songs of your homecoming that echo through creation. There is not one, who will left behind to suffer in dark illusions of despair and loveless dreams.

The child that is sleeping is God's own. Thus, I show you once again your true function here. Join the heavenly realms in celebrating the return of Christ through His Scribe. God, Our Father, has His Archangels watching over all of humanity. Their gentle care and tending are stirring in each One the memory of Home. –Father–

Our Father Who Art Within

Our Father, here within me now, there is no other
Source. I will be quiet, and let your Love fill me now.
I am now aware, the world I created is not the one
I want. I created outside my Father's will, and have
found myself in fitful dreams. This need not be, and
so I choose again. The Peace of God is within me
now, as I remember the Source of life from Love. ...
Father? ...

The eternal realm is calling for your remembrance.
What can I say to you? It is waiting for you. Imagine
the Joy you will feel when you recognize your, eternal Soul. - Father –

"I give the miracles, I have received." Rev. Pam ACIM CC Lesson
159

Eternity is in the Moment
"Into His presence would I enter Now." Rev. Pam ACIM CC Lesson
157

I seek for you in your dark illusions. Can you see the lamp lit
at your feet? It is mine. I left it there for you to find my footprints in the dust beneath your feet. Open your ears, you will
hear the brush of my sandals on the floor of the dwelling place,
you have imprisoned yourself in. Come, join with me. I will
show you the way Home. I am Shepherd to many, but I seek for
the One. Heed my call, for it is my voice you hear. Enter the
loveliness of creation and become aware of its eternal bless-

ings. The Love is right in front of you.

You dear, lovely Ones, you keep tripping over it. Do not be fooled by your illusions. Find Love in the content. There is not going to be a child more Holy than the One who stands before you. Love will not be purer than it is right now in this moment. Why do you wait for a place called heaven to Love your brother? Why the waiting? Why the delay? I am not arguing with myself when I tell you, "you never left", but still you wait for death. Your egos have convinced you that you must die to find heaven but I am telling you, you must begin to live in full awareness, to see what is right in front of you. Mortality will cease to be real to you once you open your hearts to the Love before you. I am not the maker of fantasies. I have told you of the treachery of the ego. Awareness of it will help you unlatch the harness. -Father-

"Finding the present is finding the gift." Claire ACIM OE CC 2017

I have said before, I am not here to take away from you or divide you amongst each other. I do not seek to make you unhappy. You do that enough for yourselves. If you come to me in distress, I will offer you, yourself. For, it is here we begin and end the journey to heaven. Rest assured, Love is all there is. There is no lack in God. Love lives in abundance; the ego thrives in deprivation. Let go of your errors. Give them to me. Put the faltered self on the alter and I will purify the mind that created it. Be willing to let it go. A little willingness is all it takes. Be willing to truly heal and be set free from your own agenda on what that process should look like. -Father-

"Enjoy your life. Rest in Peace." Sadhguru 2017

The Loveless Saint
"I advance only when I walk with God, not in front of Him." Lee

ACIM OE CC 2017

One can seek to understand creation and God's order, but still miss Love's presence within and the true function of their existence. Sacrifice is not necessary to find Love. The tit for tat exchanges by man for sacrifice lead away from true relationship. Love has no exchange rate. It is unlimited. Heaven is Joy. _ Father -

The ego calls to you from its loveless world to pay each other for what has always been freely given. Only, I can show you the Truth. Only, I can lead you Home. For, I am no longer fooled by the ego's illusion of the "cost" of Love. Let me lead you out and find true Peace. Heaven, but awaits your willingness. I am here with you. Follow in my footsteps and I will surely lead you Home. -Father-

"All things I cherished in the past, I have projected onto the present." Micah ACIM OE CC 2017

The Holy Light emanates from the simple, beautiful heart of God. Seek for your innocence. For, you will see it in all once you find it in yourself. The lovelessness and darkness you feel and observe is an attempt at life without recognition of its true Source. Imagine if you will a fatherless and motherless world and you are clearly viewing the ego's reality. The abandoned child is not an idea of Love. The killing and choice for war is not of the Father. Death is the ego's final, trump card in an endless game of separation and guilt.

The Son of God cannot kill what he did not create. True creation comes only from the Father and He is not a divider. Do not cherish the inconsistent mind. It offers you nothing. You will know your Father's Presence within through your own constant experience of Love. But, you must seek for what you never lost because you chose against it. Through your seeking you fulfill the prophecy of willingness that came before you. I left you the keys to heaven but you need to seek and through your willingness, you will look and see I placed them in your hand before you chose to leave, guaranteeing your safe return. -Father-

"I stand forth as the Christ of God." Masters of the Far East, Vol. 2

You see, man plays with his swords cruelly and often seeks to kill more than the just the body. Let us be clear here, the contemptable spirit has no fortunate plans for you. All forms do not leave their source without permission, you send and receive the same message in return. It is like an echo heard repetitively through the mountain canyon. It echoes and echoes, thus do your messages to your brothers echo upon their ears. -Father-

"Be excellent to each other." Rex Bear, The Leak Project, 2017

We are going to begin your reparenting process again. Within the visions of Our Father's Love, you will find your heart again. Let the visions proceed. Let yourself smile, dance and laugh. For, your Father knows of your deepest need for Love. Be brave in the face of Love. As you let go of the false, loveless past Our Father's memory of Love will be restored, and you will begin to remember only heaven. Only cherished moments of Love will remain. The cracked foundation on which you once stood is replaced. Look beneath your feet. The sands of time have disappeared. - Father -

"Christ's vision is the miracle in which all miracles are born." Rev. Pam ACIM CC

The Last Thing
"For miracles are merely change of purpose from hurt to healing."

Lee ACIM OE CC 2016

There is no difference between the fixation on the body form and the fixation of thoughts, for one leads to the other. Follow me down the path to this moment with the promise the future is not like the past. The repetitive steps you seem to be taking are leading to your final transition. It is not for man to decide the path but to simply be willing to follow my lead. Surrender to the Love within. Take upon each to recognize the One. There is no other way Home. -Father-

"Om Na Ma Ye Shu I Ah" Rajan Markose ACIM OE CC 2016

Please, my brothers, surrender to each other. Look within. Look at what is written on your hearts. At this time, you must express your true humanity which is an expression of Love. Ascend within and find the changeless dwelling place that remains undisturbed forever in a place in your hearts where there is no time. Reset your inner clocks back and forward to the loving acts of humanity where you see the Heart of Our Father being expressed. Stand forth and represent Love. You need not fear, for both cannot stand together as One presence. Lead your brothers to Joy, not sorrow. Do not lay guilt upon their minds for neither of you will heal. God is not in your illusions of each other. You cannot find Love where it is not. Only the Love within is complete and can be shared without the recourse of the ego. -Father-

"Seek the face of God and He will send His protectors." Dr. Rob ACIM OE 2016

Look upon the Holy World with the kind eyes of a child. There is no need to wait on the Master. For, He always comes when the night is cold. His Light exudes warmth, filling the cold, inner spaces of your heart with the heat of Love. Do not believe the night and seeming, eternal darkness will consume you. For I have come at last. You will awaken with the dawn and I will not leave your mind again. As your eyes open, you will find, my Light does not hurt them. Gentle sounds will meet your ears and Joy will fill your heart. So, do not be afraid of the come what may. -Father-

"God's will is for your perfect happiness and of this you can be certain. To align your will with God's is but to make this certain state your home. This is but a granting of a wish come true, and when it is all you wish for it will come to be. And, in the granting of this wish will come your rest and the laying down of every heavy burden you have carried." Mari Perron, A Course of Love

... Stay in the Good, and Pray ...

CHAPTER TWO

The Betrayal

I walk with you. I stand beside you in acknowledgement that seeking for Love outside your own heart leads to this bitter disappointment. -Father-

Checkmate

"I am under no laws but Gods." Rev. Pam ACIM CC Lesson 76

Eventually, though you strain much, you find yourself in an impossible situation with seemingly no way out. In the game of chess, the queen, the heart of the game covers the most ground and from multiple angles. Love is indeed protective of Truth, for they are integral parts of one another. The King (Truth) is protected by the Love of his entire court. Checkmate only occurs through loss. Do not be despondent in hopes that it will further your development. Self-inflicted penalties of any kind are unwarranted. There are no errors that will not be used as spiritual correctives. The innocent child is seeking for its Home. Let me set you free, let me be your consistent Joy. God is good, and all good things are of Him. It is truly a good thing, your ego consistently finds itself in checkmate, for its demise is your final victory. I maintain the final move in this or any of the ego's death games, for I am a God of Love and I created the piece the hand rests on. As you learn, your gratitude toward me will grow and you will come to honor Our Father and learn of our great power and strength through Him. -Father-

"God is in the wastebasket, for God is in my mind." Micah ACIM OE CC 2017

There is Love inside of you. At the core of your existence is your energy Source. Your life Source is Love. It is the life energy, sustaining every cell of your form. Love is the life force of all things ever created from a single thought of Love. You are the Love you seek. You contain the All. You are not here to convince with your words this is true. You are here to represent through loving action that God is all there is. That indeed, Love is real and sustains All. God, Our Father is not in form, for no form could ever contain the All. -Father-

"Christ is in me and where He is God must be, for Christ is part of Him." ACIM OE Chapter 8:XI:106

The perfect Peace of God lies within every man's heart but awaiting recognition. The blessed Peace of Our Father remains, though, forgotten. Let me help you remember your identity. We will recreate a more solid identity for you. The soul does not need restoration, but the personality structure is indeed need of help. Let go of idols made of fear, for this is the cornerstone upon which we will rebuild a more comfortable, loving, eternal existence. -Father-

I have never been in favor of suffering in any form. Let us, deliver you soon. I can and will abolish your ego as soon as you are willing. God in His great mercy finds us perfect still. For, His Love is pure and tender. In times of distress, ask for my help and I will send comfort. Not the kind of comfort you have offered to yourself time and time again. I offer you what your five senses cannot provide. Life is so unpredictable, so uncanny, so full of fate for you. I offer you, your release from these endless cycles. Do not ignore my call to you, for I offer you, your greatness. -Father-

"I am out of the correction business and into the healing business." Lee ACIM OE CC

Under the Wings of His Protection

"Steady our feet Father, let our doubts be quiet and our Holy Minds be still and speak to us. We have no words to give to you. We would but, listen to your word and make it our ours. Lead our practicing as does a Father lead a little child along a way he does not understand. Yet, does he follow, sure that he is safe because his Father leads the way for him." Rev. Pam ACIM CC Review 5:2

Christ shines forth from the cradle of humanity tawaiting recognition. Our Father is ostentatious in His Love of His Child. His displays of Love are "stellar" in a most literal fashion. The universe is the Holy Child's playground. The relationship between Our Father and His Child is spiritually magnetic. When the wills are in proper alignment, the joining is instantaneous. The alignment of the wills, aligns minds, thereby aligning the purpose. Living in congruence with the Divine is Divine Joy, for Love produces immense Joy. I cannot emphasis enough to you my dear brothers the need for your commitment to let yourselves be released. -Father-

"Abide in me, as I Abide in you." Rev. Regina Dawn Akers, The Teachings of the Inner Ramana

God is in the inner most part of every living being. Our Father is not hiding from you. Look upon the blameless child and find him looking back at you with wide eyes of acceptance. Wide eyed and shameless does the innocent child enter heaven's remembrance. Worry not, I am preparing you for this final step. Let go of ideas of guilt, shame and blame you have placed on yourself, for it is necessary they be removed. I stand here beside you, offering you the return to your innocence. I am here gently holding your hand. With your other hand, reach out to the child standing beside me. Look, it is you. Let yourself embrace this child. Hold him close to your chest and feel the remembrance of Love. You will find Our Father here within your innocence. -Father-

"Do not try to look beyond yourself for the Truth. The Truth is inside you." Lee ACIM OE CC

The Lullaby of Our Mother
"He is Us" Dr. Rob ACIM OE CC 2016

In the heavens within, I swell in the vast spaces of your heart. I can be heard in the laughter of children when they play. I am the first Home of Love. I dwell within you all as I am the original Mother. Within, you will find the Truth of your existence. You do not need more illusions. Just close your eyes and listen to the lullaby. The is no such thing as separation for you anymore. Can you feel the Oneness within? Everyone is here. Everything you see reflects a higher plane of existence. The is no reality to be found in a dream, only reflections of higher realities.

Once you wake, you will become aware of more planes of existence in the Oneness. You cannot find presence in sentient reflections of a greater Truth. Yet, you are not the first to hear the call of heaven. Just simply listen to the lullaby of Our Mother as she calls us home. Her presence will heal your heart. I am not here to tell you it will be easy to be a Scribe of the Truth of Love. Every night you dream of Home. You must rest from your illusions. Some of them are mind boggling. Let Love happen today.   -Father-

"God Is." Rev. Pam ACIM CC

The Chalice of Redemption
"I am not a body, I am not even the mind'. Isha Kriya

When I offer you the Chalice of Salvation, I offer you the All of corrected thought. God offers you more than your form can provide. Holding onto form and not seeing God as present within, is surely death. For, the unquenchable thirst can never be satisfied, if man seeks for God where He is not. The special relationship signifies the division you placed before yourself as a substitution for Truth and Love. You look to each other, not knowing you are seeking for control. The Master, understands your quandary and looks with compassion, recognizing only the rebirth out of form and into conscious existence. Form, without conscious awareness of Source, is a true disaster and a state the ego structure cherishes deeply.

God, in His Divine Mercy finds us perfect still. In His sight, you remain as a constant in His creation. Therefore, your return to awareness of this constancy is sure. The Chalice of Redemption is offered up to the child who believes he is, but a fleeting thought of God. But, God has no fleeting thoughts. All His creation proceeds from clear intention. There are no mistakes, for there are none in God. Man, only believes in temporary conditions because he has allowed his ego to convince him, he is temporary. This is easy to do, as deep in the inner regions of man's heart, he knows, without his Source clearly intact, life cannot be sustained. -Father-

"Unless, I side with the Truth in my brother and "side with him", I cannot be grateful for him." Lee ACIM OE CC

The ego seeks to become that source. The mad exchanges begin at once. When I went into the desert for forty days and nights, I was attempting to show you the consistent answer you must return to the ego structure. Your ego will offer you the whole world in exchange for your eternal reality. Its endless desires and exchanges offer you nothing. There is no container for Love. Remember, God remains in His Holy temple within your heart. Let us look for this constant Source of life together. I will show you the unimaginable glory you truly hold within. Give this promise back to yourself. We start with the Love you have denied yourself in every relationship you hold dear. Allow loving moments to be given you. Stand present with each brother in every moment of exchange and extend Love. - Father-

"Past, present and future are not continuous unless we force continuity." Lee ACIM OE CC

You made the concept of temporary existence and have frightened yourselves. What could be more terrifying than to believe at some point, you will take your last breath and cease to exist. What a farce and what an impossible position you have placed yourselves in. In Truth, you do not hold the answer to this terrifying result of egoic thought, but I do. I will lead you out of your dismay and into the Light. -Father-

"Salvation is the end of specialness." Rev. Pam ACIM CC

The Horse Race
"Get off the cross, we need the wood." Paula ACIM OE CC 2016

Welcome the change of perspective that Love is real, and it can bring in its coming. The Eternal and the finite cannot both be true. Cast off the illusions you no longer want. Do not engage your ego, for it simply has no way of winning the race. It is like, unto a horse in a race with blinders on. You have no idea who is running beside you. It is all guess work of who's feet belong to whom. Seriously, be careful who you allow to ride on your back and guide you to the finish line. Much time will be saved in the race, and more than mere seconds, if you let me be your guide Home. – Father –

"My mind holds only what I think with God." Rev. Pam ACIM CC Review IV

The Dispensation of Thought Forms
"The healing moment is now." Lee ACIM OE CC

Thought forms of cherished, replayed memories are some of the most difficult to remove. The ego has convinced you, salvation lies in the past. Indeed, you have come to believe the present moment is bereft of Joy. The guilt, ridden mind will not allow the gift of Peace to enter. It replays endless versions of the same illusion, looking for the release from guilt through a myriad of self-inflicted punishments. For, the ego wants man to remain on the cross replaying the scenario of self-sacrifice. -Father –

"If I defend myself, I am attacked." Rev. Pam ACIM CC 135

The illusion that sacrifice brings salvation, puts the Son of God at odds with himself. For in sacrifice, there must be the guilty and the innocent. How can the Son of God be both? We are welcome to seek for home where we choose. The framework of your illusions will begin to fall away through your willingness to choose again. In this choice, to look beyond the dream your ego displays before you, lies the decision for heaven's memory to return. I cannot stress enough the importance of the daily practice of silence. The criteria for healing you have placed before yourselves often gets over complicated by your ego's need for control. No matter, I will simplify the process by lifting the veil obscuring your sight. You will not find Peace in this world, for the ego knows nothing of Peace. – Father –

"Sickness is a defense against the Truth." Rev. Pam ACIM CC 136

I am going to begin a deep, cleansing. This process will cleanse your mind of emotional distractions. You are loved, and your efforts are recognized and appreciated. The whole is lifted by the One. Trust and together we will eliminate the distress and you will become more comfortable and less disturbed. Cleansing is necessary. Old, belief systems, deeply rooted in the reactive mind can lead to despondence. Let us work on the relationship with your earthly father. I will lift your awareness and then clear the karmic return, freeing you both from having to revisit this principle. Forgiveness abounds. God is good. Love is real. - Father -

Ant Hill
"Eternity has already started." Laurie ACIM OE CC 2018

I am the singer of the Love songs of all mankind. I, but represent the One Son, standing before Him with Love and Truth in his heart. Join, if you will, in manifesting this Love before Our Father, through the Love and forgiveness of your brother. Truly, how does one go back to when the hatred began? Who killed whom in Truth, or is this when the fallacy began, you were finite and capable of such mightiness? Man cannot destroy what God, Our Father created. No matter how great he is, an ant moving a mound of dirt only looks mighty to other ants, but most certainly not to the ant eater. – Father –

"All idols are the false ideas I made that have arisen in a gap, I think exists between the Truth and my awareness. These are the false ideas that torment me so." Lee ACIM OE CC

The Prodigal's Son
"I whisper to God my Father, and I am undisturbed." Masters of the Far East Vol#3 Pg. 40

"For God so loved the world that he gave His only begotten Son ..." and His Son was answered when he called, allowed to believe he was just a body, and he began searching outside of himself for Love. It is like, unto a teenager, who leaves his mother's arms in search of the same, deep Love and never finds it. But, this must be allowed, or the son will flounder in his footsteps. He will never challenge himself to create anything truly. Since the separation, it is a natural process in the development of the Son of God, to enter illusions in search of Love.

Not realizing his mother is so loving because of her extension of Love, the son seeks to be filled, instead of extending. The separation from the Source of life can be seen in the illusion as the mother and child. At first, the choice for separation is revealed through lack of fulfillment, which then becomes rebellion. The return from rebellion is often long and tedious with many errors. The Father knows the Son will eventually return. So, He waits patiently. You must do for your brother, what your Father has done for you. Why? Because it is extension. -Father-

"I will not hurt myself again today." Rev. Pam ACIM CC Lesson 330

Today in time, I give my heart to you. I stand before you once again in time to tell you, I Love you ... Here in time, it is only a whisper, but in heaven's ear it is a Song of Prayer. Gratitude is in my heart today, you are finally lifting your eyes toward My presence in your heart. I am thankful for today's lesson. - Father –

"God is my Source, and yours, we cannot see apart from him. I am One with my Holy Father. He lives within us all and is indeed Us." Rev. Pam ACIM CC

God is in His Holy Temple
"I will there be Light" Rev. Pam ACIM CC Lesson 73

You cannot direct your own process. Through your willingness is your Peace restored. You do not have to grasp for heaven, for your grasp is limited by what you think it is. I cannot restore the wholeness of Truth and Love within the parameters you have set for me. There are three aspects of the human mind, you do not yet understand. These three aspects were inverted by the ego: Source, mind and form. Because of this inversion, man has come to believe he is alone and destined to die. The bottom-up ended thought systems of the ego keeps you stuck in illusions of Love. You have come to believe the only way out of your misery is through death. But you are not tortured by your body, for it is a neutral thing. -Father-

"Blessed are you who know beforehand about what may entrap you, and who flee what is alien to you." The Secret Teachings of Jesus, The Book of Thomas, Chapter 9

You are restless and frightened by your mind and its selected thought forms. It is essential you come to recognize the inverted platform you are attempting to escape and its resultant ideas you continue to act upon. I cannot repair the inversion within if it is not recognized. The ego relies on its hidden autonomy within this agenda. You are free to choose always which voice to listen to. I have no alternate agenda. Truth does not need to be cloaked in hidden, derisive plans. It is straight-forward and knows of innocence. Truth is an active, healing thought derived directly from the Heart of Our Loving God. -Father-

"What is Dying For?" Rev. Harrison ACIM OE CC 2017

The limited, body form, but represents limited concepts in your mind. The death of bodies is only perceived as "so" by those still in bodies. For the "dying", death is a quick, transient experience. It takes, but a Holy Instant and your memory returns. For in this moment, you have remembered all the answered "whys". For those who choose to turn away from Love's presence will return to be witnesses of their own egoic ideas of life's source. The return to Love is the only concept being challenged in death. The Holy Instant is the return to Love's presence, whether form ceases its perceived function or continues to vibrate is irrelevant. It is, and always has been about the return to your awareness and acceptance of being "in" Love. For the Light of heaven is, but pure emanations of Love. The mere glimpses you choose to receive while in the body move to a constant within your new sight in heaven. -Father-

"The peace of God is shining in me now. Let all things shine upon me in that peace and let me bless them with the Light in me." Rev. Pam ACIM CC Lesson 188

You will not find Peace in this world, for the ego knows nothing of Peace. Man thinks he can correct the outer world while the inner world remains unknown.

"The ego calls for vengeance, the heart calls for Love." Lee ACIM OE CC

35

Review the special relationship. Invite me into the relationship. Let yourself process the feelings of inadequacy. I will replace them. Do you see how the ego places you in impossible scenarios? You can only be one body at a time, and yet there seems to be an impossible requirement to be more than one. Change the content to the Love of Our Father. The temporary existence and shifting realities of your illusions offer you no promise of Love or Peace. You project the fearful content you see. "Let all things be as they are", in each blessed moment. Remember, Goodness and God are One. Let there be no lack in each moment. Remember, the strength of the Joy you contain which emanates from Love's presence between you. -Father-

"Betrayal is when I hold a grievance against my brother, because he has not become what I wanted him to be." Lee ACIM OE CC

I Enter Now
"You can't teach what you don't know. You can't lead where you won't go." Stephen of God ACIM OE CC 2015

Let me enter your quiet moments. Come, sit by the stream of stillness. I have many things to speak to you of. God enters only when welcome. So many get lost in thinking they must stop movement to find the stillness. I assure you, I understand your restlessness, for I was a man prone to move about. I found stillness in the long walks I took and the endless crafts I would enjoy in moments of solitude. I often occupied my hands while speaking to the masses. I allowed my hands and body to be an expression of Divine, creative principles. I laughed much among my friends, for I knew of the importance of joyful moments. The written books do not speak much of our fun and laughter as we became true Brothers of the Light with one unified purpose. Oh, we had our disputes, but Love was always the answer. I am often asked to speak of my journey in this moment. So, as it is in the Oneness, we join and lift the roof once again. Come join with us in the bliss of the brotherhood that can only come through joining in Love and Truth. -Father-

"To all that speaks of terror, answer thus; I will forgive, and this will disappear." Lee ACIM OE CC 2017

Something More Important
"Reality is never frightening." Lee ACIM OE CC

Dear Holy Child; the veil is but, so, very thin now as you have become willing to see clearly through the new lens, the Truth of your existence. I, but stand on the other side of the door you have attempted to close, offering you my hand. Come walk with me awhile, let us laugh at the folly of the ego you are overcoming. Look within. My communication is direct, yet gentle. I will show you a Light so pure within you, at first you will weep at its gentleness. Indeed, it might be hard to ac-knowledge it. It is, the one experience that seems at first too good to be true. The ego structure wants you to believe, all happiness is "to good to be true". That indeed, Joy is but a fleet-ing experience. So, as it stands, to you the awakening seems slow and tedious. Some things I give, I give just to you in the healing process. For, they are tailored just for you. Yes, it is all that specific and yet, simple as the answer is always Love. -Father-

"Love, is the way I walk in gratitude." Rev. Carl ACIM CC 2017

God is here. If you but recognized this you would be free of the conflict. Therefore, your willingness is necessary. The choice for God cannot be made through coercion because Love knows only of free choice. - Father -

Prayer of the Footprints

I know only of the Christ who resides within my heart. Faithfully, I follow Thee down the path you would have me take. Other paths contain mirages of happiness and fulfillment.

If I, but steady my feet in the promise of Truth and the heart of Love, I will always see your footprints on the path you would have me take. For, You, always keep your promises. You, my Father know no other way. I can always look to my heart and find You.

For, I did not know we were truly One, until I awoke from my slumber and found You still here with me. For, though the whole world had vanished from my sight, you remained.

And now, I but recognize what has always been True. We, You and I, are indeed One. -Father-

"I will there be Light." Rev. Pam ACIM CC Lesson 73

The Forced Contest

"My Home awaits me. I will hasten there." Rev. Pam ACIM CC Lesson 226

The ego has no way of knowing which way the tides will turn in its endless, myriad of envisioned outcomes. This confusion factor keeps the mind in chaos, trying to choose the "best outcome". Thoughts fly through the mind in partial format, forcing the mind to compete with itself in a contest for the "best" outcome in selected relationships and situations. Peace is impossible within the contest and the ego keeps the individual's mind seeking endlessly for Peace where it cannot be found. God is in His Holy Temple where thought ceases and true learning begins. -Father-

"Be ye observer." Secret Teachings of Jesus, Gospel of Thomas

Give all things back to our Father. For, what is askew will be absorbed into the aqueous. God is the complete embodiment of righteousness. Do not be fooled by the ego's displays of "right and wrong". Turn your confusion over to the One, Holy Mind we share with Him, who contains Us All as One Holy Child. Our Father does not exist within any thought boundaries. The purity of His Light contains no shadows. His Truth is known at once. His Love knows of no bitterness or regret. All these concepts dissolve at once in Love's presence. The Truth is seen everywhere and in all facets of time. All illusions are dissolved and only the Love in their creation will remain eternally. -Father –

"Let mercy come to you more quickly." Lee ACIM OE CC

The Restoration of the Child
"The past is over, it can touch me not." Rev. Pam ACIM CC Lesson 289

The Light within is obscured only by the filters of egoic thought. It is difficult for man to imagine, his mind is the cause of his distress. What he fails to see; it is his interpretation of his world that is so disturbing to his Peace of mind. I have fulfilled my promise and completed the restoration process within my heart. You cannot follow one who does not demonstrate the proper function of mankind. The kingdoms of the ego are tempting indeed, but the Holy Child must remember, cause and effect are one movement. A kingdom built on a false premise will surely fall, for this is always the outcome of temporal ideology. Only Our Father within holds the master plan that herald's eternity. -Father-

"I am looking through the dream window." Micah ACIM OE CC 2017

Next Coffin Please

"Damnation is your judgement on yourself. Judgement will always give you a false direction" Sam ACIM OE CC 2017

I bring you Peace and Joy. Concepts of death remain as an ever-tightening noose around the neck of mankind. For, everyone who believes in this finality, remains terrified. At this juncture in the timeline of humanity, man is testing this concept in his threat of the total annihilation of his planetary home. So, as you witness this destructive concept play out, remember the divided mind from which all these distortions arise. I cannot stress enough, the importance of seeking inner guidance at this time. The Holy Mind is a resource of Peace in troubled times. God remains constant. - Father -

His Love is pouring forth upon your hearts. Be the compassion and Love, humanity is in desperate need of. Love transcends all concepts of war and death. The man child is playing with his book of matches, terrifying himself and all who have no memory of Home. Remember Home for them. Keep Love and Truth on your minds, so you can pour it forth upon the desperate hearts seeking for comfort. Pray for all who come to you seeking for the answer among the chaos. Remember, there is not a right or wrong side in war. All sides are demonstrating the ego's love of self-destruction. Stand forth and offer the cup of redemption to your brother, for it truly is the only answer. - Father-

Let us review what you have learned ... You do not want death. The solution, you will see is so, very simple here. Ask Our Father, above and within, for the Holy, Eternal Mind. Bury the concepts of death and its caskets in your ego's graveyard. I have spoken before of the way you should walk amongst your brothers. They truly believe they can kill "all life" with their toy matches. Eternal life is truly real. No matter how many times, nor the many ways you imagine this can be done, it is a ridiculous fallacy.

The instant mass death occurs, mass life occurs simultaneously. The look upon your faces as you awaken, is by far one of the most blessed events the human Soul can experience. The end of your darkened illusions is indeed a celebration of great Joy. Let man light his match. Only the ego would try to kill itself. Choose for the eternal One. Receive the message, there is no such thing as mass extinction, without mass awakening. You see child, the Son of God chose for the illusion of form over eternal life. The extra-ordinary thing is, the ego's format for "life" is chosen for again and again. Once your mind's descent into form without God was complete, the ego began to play a losing game called death ... next coffin please. - Father-

"Woe to you, for you have not learned the lesson ..., that they rise from death!" The Secret Teachings of Jesus, The Book of Thomas, Chapter 9

Ego the finite: The separation of true identity
"You can but hurt yourself." Lee ACIM OE CC

It is through the acknowledgement of our errors, the Holy Spirit's correction is offered up. This correction offers healing at multiple levels and in multiple directions at once. You cannot escape the consequences of your errors without Divine intervention. The "Law of Karma" is the law of the ego. Would you punish your child for tripping while learning to walk? Probably not. You, mostly likely would offer him your hands to steady his gate, providing stability to his strengthening legs. Remember, you are this child to m e. I do not see you as the grown-up you think you are. I see your innocence in all things great and small. I love you, in the name of Our Father within. – Father –

The Train Wreck

"Do not board the train." Lee ACIM OE CC

Thought without action is indeed meaningless. Action brings forward the change in direction of the thought. Do not act if your thoughts are disturbing to you, for then you will see unfortunate movement in the path laid before you. I will not return to you a lie for the Truth. This indeed, would be disturbing to you and would be an inversion of the Divine Laws of Providence, which could only belong to the ego's inverted understanding of Truth and its function.
– Father –

"I give away what I do not value." Lee ACIM OE CC

God the Infinite: The True Identity

"The Holy Mind of God is within." Chris ACIM OE CC 2017

Love yourself through the Christ you see in me until you can see it in yourself, for we are One Love. It is with great Joy I express this Truth to you, dear Child. God Our, Holy Father has blessed us as His, Holy Child. We are His precious Child. His Love is immense. He created an entire universe for His Child to play in. There are no errors, only lessons. He looks upon what is precious to Him with a gentle smile. "Uh oh, you might not want to go that way as you might fall down and skin your knee." The Holy Spirit is the bandaid to the scrape. It will heal in the Presence of Love.

The finite is of no consequence to Him who does not see it. He will let you play and if you call to Him, He will pick you up and

comfort you through the Holy Spirit within your heart. God will bless you back for every blessing you extend to His creation, for He made it for you and loves to see you happy. I will end it there. Heaven is a state of Love and Joy is its result. God bless you dear, Holy Child. For, His blessing extends to all of creation through you. Hmmm... what a blessing it is to be His Child.
- Father-

It is within, we find each other. You cannot find God when you seek for Love in separate containers. Look inside your hearts and you will find what you have been looking for. Can you see me sitting there beside you? Return these words to the Father within and reestablish your True Identity in Him. Give all things back to Our Father and miracles will abound before your Holy Sight. Love is our power as His Holy Son. We are One. Let go of trying to establish your identity through the vessel containing your Holy Soul. This is the Loving Answer. - Father-

"All dissonance is harmony misunderstood." Wendy ACIM OE CC 2016

The Hands upon the Eyes
"Some people are blind in one eye and can't see out of the other." Dad Riding 1979

The blind, stay blind until they ask for Sight, as demonstrated at the pool of waters in the New Testament of the Holy Grail. The blind man seeks new sight through the teacher standing before him. – Father –

"Christ's vision turns darkness into Light." Rev. Pam ACIM CC Lesson 302

The Broken Tablet
"Look for heaven under every rock." Dr. Rob ACIM OE CC 2016

Man's mind is like a broken tablet, one piece divided into two disjointed sides. Our Father, Who Art in the Heaven within, is the primary, energy Source that contains you. He stands ever present in all creation in every particulate of energy and form. The order in creation, its perfect self-containment and ever evolving forms, represent to our senses what can also be found within for, indeed, this is where it begins, ends and begins again. You cannot find a more perfect solution than the evolvement of all spiritual concepts and all their formal counterparts of thought and form. The mind displays its thought systems upon the cascading, back drop of creation. As you willingly let go of your illusions and let me replace them with true vision, all things will become Holy within your sight. Not because the backdrop has changed, but because you have changed your mind and chosen for God. -Father-

"I am just a living witness that you can be an imperfect solider and still be fighting for God Almighty. Don't think you gotta be perfect, cause, I ain't." C. Allen Adams 2017

There is nothing you need do but, be willing to receive the Revelation. The choice for darkness is replaced by the choice for Light and Love. Blessed is the child who sees the proper teacher. The flashy toys and ploys your ego places before your eyes seem tempting indeed. But, the darkness beneath the shiny surface of illusions soon consumes the mind and the inversion of Truth begins to churn the mind, sending it on an endless search for Love and Peace. Rest easy in the Holy Spirit's care, for the Holy Light cannot be extinguished and shines away all the ego's disastrous plans for you. -Father-

Trust in the path I lay before you. Remember, I have walked the corridors of the ego's deluded mind and have found my Soul's release. I am not blind to its argument for death and the fearful, spiritual desert the Son of God finds himself in as a result. Let me be your guide out of this seeming misery and into the Love and Peace of Our Father, Who Art in the Heaven within you each blessed moment. -Father-

"Blessed are you, who weep and are afflicted by those without hope, for you will be released from all that binds you." The Secret Teachings of Jesus, The Book of Thomas

I await your acceptance of the Truth within your hearts. Once this new reality is within your sight, you will finally understand the fallacy you have been believing so whole-heartedly, you became drunk with your own solutions for your salvation. Our Father within, stands above these illusions through His dispensation of the sacred knowledge through His, Holy Spirit, residing in the Holy heart of every brother you encounter. Remember, I have said before, we are of One Mind. This mind is sustained through the Holy Spirit residing in every heart. I have not left your side, nor placed the chasm you see between us. God, Our, Holy Father does not look at His Son from a distance. The choice was made at the beginning of the Son's query outside of himself, the Father placed His Holy Spirit within His Son's heart, sustaining the essence of Heaven, His true Home, where only Love resides. -Father-

"Only Love sails straight from the harbor, and only Love will lead us to the other side." Wynonna, Only Love

... Stay in the Good and Pray .

CHAPTER THREE

The Crucifiction

It is over, but you do not know it. So, I send you visions of your resurrection to remind you to look within for hope. I am the Love you seek and I will not forsake you. -Father-

Trust Yourself, Trust God
"I love to bow." Rev. Regina Dawn Akers 2017

Many want to own, few want to Love. Let it all go to truly gain the aptitude of the Holy Son of God. Trust fall into the grace of God. Only the ego believes the limited few are to inherit the Kingdom of God. They look to the skies for what lies within. Extend the Light inward and find heaven awaiting your recognition, for what it shines on it illuminates. -Father-

"I'm taking the high watch today." Wendy ACIM CC OE 2017

The Taming of the Shrew
"Help me Holy Father to heal from this insanity. Heal my babies, heal my heart-mind." Anna 2015

Despite its appearance, this is not victimization, but a refusal to see clearly the current state of your brother's mind. You went through a continuous, non-stop war. No solider is asked to endure battles of this length dear child. Have mercy on yourself. Your brother is momentarily insane. Understand, he may not heal in this lifetime. Release him and let him go his way. You cannot help those who will not help themselves. Go inward and let us begin to heal your inner world and the outer world will correct accordingly. Love yourself, for we are One. Leave for God, what is Gods to do. Let this world go for a while and find rest. - Father -

Do not try to correct the illusion. It cannot be corrected, for it is born out of insanity. The unregenerate soul is savage. The ego maintains, the defeat of one's brother is gain. It is an endless, feeding frenzy. It is, life without God. The dark abyss that must be recognized in this world, lies in the mind. The ego convinces man, the greatest Love lies outside himself. So, you seek for Love outside of yourselves no matter the quality of the source. Child, you cannot heal the unwilling. Those who lie to themselves and the world will not find Peace. Do not let your ego destroy your Love. You owe no explanation to any man. Do not hide in a garden of explanations. Be free to be wherever you are. -Father-

"The loss of totality is the loss of reality." Lee ACIM OE CC

I weep for the children of God. I rock them gently in the arms of all that is true. I offer hope. I offer Peace of mind. I offer you, yourselves. Open your eyes and wake from your slumber oh, Holy Children of the first thought of Love. Once you wake, you will cry no more. You will be washed clean of your darkened dreams of despair. Listen to the Holy Mind for it contains the answer to every question mankind will ever pose. The Sonship grows stronger when you remember who you are. You must hold your identity out for All. Extend your hand to the weary ones. There are no Angels without God. There are none in humanity without God. The choice to be whole again is their own. The choice is not yours to make for them. Yesterday is gone. The separation was decided for by man. The Son of God is lonely by choice, not by force. -Father-

The Little White Lie
"Holiness cannot be contained." Laurie ACIM OE CC 2018

Look down Child. Do you not see the sands of time beneath your feet you have chosen to stand upon? The shifting sands are confusing your mind. Let yourself fall into the vortex of the quicksand of time. Let go, of all you think your understanding gave you of "reality". The Truth does not wax and wane like the moon in your sight. Truth is a constant. The addition and subtraction are done by the egoic mind as an act of mere convenience. It truly thinks it can accomplish this and does not see the folly in trying to quantify Love and Truth, as it dictates your reality. I am not fooled by this, for I stand above the ego's playground. - Father -

The struggle begins with the concept, there are variations of the Truth. This is your ego's "little white lie". A glaring example of this error is demonstrated in the ego's concept of murder. That, indeed, it is an acceptable concept to "kill" thousands or millions with one missile, but it is seen as carnage and reprehensible to act this out on an individual basis. Where is the logic in this upside, down thinking? Indeed, there is none. The ego is seeking to qualify Truth; indeed, it is different depending on the level of murder. Mass murder is acceptable, but you "must not kill". How can both be True? It is clear the masses do not see the fallacy of this thought system. -Father-

"Your forgiveness entitles you to vision." Lee ACIM OE CC

The Error Within
"Watch what Love can do sweet Sister." Jesus 2017

"Jesus Loves me this I know." But, dear child, do you really know? The magnitude of the Love I offer you inside is skewed only by the lack of true Love you have for yourself. Look at the child sitting next to you. Do you see the innocence, you, yourself contain? Open your eyes and let yourself take in the innocence you see there. It is the "real" Love of heaven you are looking upon. Children are wide eyed with acceptance without any judgement whatsoever. For, within their eyes you see the innocence of the heavenly realms you will eventually return to. Exploration without judgement is only available to those who do not judge. - Father -

I offer you release by pointing out to you the Chalice of Redemption, standing before you and the innocent Love the Chalice contains. Can you not see whom and what stands before you, who would condone the rape and slaughter of innocence? But, I remind you, take rein of your judgements of those who have chosen for this through action. For, every act of betrayal against your own innocence is the same choice against God the Father within, who's primary emanation is Love and innocence.

God is in His Holy Temple within each one of you. Do not seek to slaughter your own innocence. Look at the wide-eyed, loving trust children display before you and find yourself there. God is merciful and those who will pause for a moment and look within will find a child still standing there in the innocence and Love. In its purest form, there is truly nothing that can destroy the eternal Love, beckoning to each one of us.

The child within you is not capable of judgement and the resulting self-inflicted punishments you then rain down upon your brothers. The error within, is not the result of your brother's hatred, but your own projected, self-hatred. Therefore, we, together must take a close look at your heart, and the shame and guilt clogging its arteries. I cannot free you of illusions you insist on holding onto. The putrid poisons of egoic thought must be cleared and though this is hard to look upon, it is necessary for true freedom and the return of Love's flow through the chambers of your heart. -Father-

"When you pray, you will find rest, for you have left pain and abuse behind. When you leave bodily pains and passions, you will receive rest from The Good One, and you will reign with the King, you united with the King and the King united with you, now and for ever and ever. Amen." The Secret Teachings of Jesus, The Book of Thomas, Chapter 9:6

The Divine Secret Garden
"Christ is the vision I will use today" Rev. Pam ACIM CC Lesson 271

I come to you to soften your heart and make way for heaven's return. In the deepest recesses of your being there is a scared space designed just for you. Let us take a walk through this Holy place where you will find the trees bearing the fruits of your spiritual labor, born forth in all their sweetness. The unripened fruits have sweetened with the nectar of Love. Gone, is the bitterness that once laid upon your lips. The rank taste of the ego cannot be upon your tongue in Love's awareness. Let us take a journey and gaze upon the waters, nourishing the secret Holy garden of your soul. Take a drink of the luminous, living waters I am offering to you dear One. Let yourself imbibe in these eternal waters of remembrance and Be Ye Restored by the sweetness of the Love they contain. Heaven awaits your return here. Your ego would like you to focus on the thorns and not the soft, radiant petals of the flower. It, but represents in correspondence, the painful thorns the ego uses to distract you from your Divine Identity. You are the flower, not the thorns. Cup your hands around this flower in all its radiant beauty and take in its majesty. -Father-

"God, is the ultimate Cause in reality." Rev. Harrison ACIM OE CC 2018

The Lilies of the Christ
"No one can give what he has not received." Rev. Pam ACIM CC Lesson 159

You call upon your brother for Love but, what if he has not given and received much Love in his illusions. Maybe, he is cut off from his internal Source in his present awareness. In this case, your brother becomes a bitter disappointment to you. You seek him to fill your cup. Yet, you are both living in illusions of Love outside yourselves. Is it any wonder you get confused? Go within. -Father-

Let us consider for a moment, the lily. It has a fragrance equal to the rose, but without the thorny stings you have offered yourself through the idea, only one type of flower is contained in the garden of Heaven. Indeed, you have learned from the rose bush to release your grasp of Love and let me show you the flower that offers forgiveness and Love born of true relationship. I have not forgotten the garden I wept in, nor the lilies born in forgiveness planted there for all of humanity. So, to are the lilies of forgiveness springing up in your Soul's garden. These are the same lilies I offer to you from my sacred garden. For, all forgiveness is born from the same Divine Love you all contain. -Father-

"Jesus said, 'Let one who seeks not stop seeking until one finds. When one finds, one will be disturbed. When one is disturbed, one will be amazed, and will reign over all." The Secret Teachings of Jesus, The Gospel of Thomas

The Killing Field 10/12/2017, 2 am

"The song of redemption is echoing through all of the corridors of this life." Lee ACIM OE CC

I will do all that needs to be done. Find Peace, find God. Man believes, he must struggle to find what has always been so. The ego presents a false reality wherein man must struggle to find identity. This is its greatest ploy against your sanity and its constant pull on man's mind to seek for the self in every container, but its own. Close your eyes to this world. You will not find what you are looking for in its myriad of illusions. How can one find Love in a loveless concept? Let us take a close, honest look at its loveless ideology. Love's equivalent is hatred. Do not fool yourself, the ego is a master of manipulation. Every Holy concept is inverted and changed to fit its agenda. What is the agenda? The answer here is simple: it seeks to kill you.

This it cannot do, but the concern here is, you believe it can. The dark night for humanity comes when the killing field surrounds it and the masses scream for mercy from the merciless. Is there not one among your leaders who will call for Love? The mercy humanity seeks, will only be found in the heart of Love they are all running away from. God, Our Father, returns His Love through His Son. The Son needs to look within to find the answer to his plight, but this he fears. The loveless child indeed would rather "die" then Love.

The ego convinces man, there is no Love in the world. This is not true. The projected content is believed and followed by the masses without question. I say to you now, question it and let the Holy Spirit's answer lead you out of the concepts of death and into the awareness of the Eternal Life which has always been yours. The Loving answers you contain are the salvation of humanity. Be the Peace. Be the Love. Be the Joy, for in this extension your brother will see another choice is possible. -Father-

"There is no death, for death is not your will." Rev. Pam ACIM CC

The Timeless Moment
"Now is the closest approximation of eternity." Rev. Reja ACIM OE CC 2017

I have whispered to you through the ages when I found peril there amongst you. But, mankind continues to place God where no Love can be found. The idols you have placed before yourselves are haunting your minds. You look to your brother for Love and find yourselves bereft. Love calls to Love, so how is it you can find Love when you have not dared to look within yourselves for Its presence? There is no need to create Love, for it already exists. Man became lonely when he began the external search for Love. So, it is in the existential reality, mankind builds his idols.

All the idols contain the same theme; what exists in the without, contains more value than that which is contained within. The ego worships and heralds the builders who have graced your planetary home and overlooks the simple man and his simple good, who's home the cradle of humanity rests. Indeed, this is the backward thought system of the ego structure, playing itself forward in humanity through its endless idolatry of form. Enter the timeless moment and find the Love and Truth waiting for you there.
-Father-

"The miracle is the first step in giving back the cause." Lee ACIM OE CC

The Pie
"The devil will tell you to rob a bank and call the police while your doing it." Bianca Carter, 2016

I await your readiness. The Holy Mind you contain is within your grasp now, but again you must let go of what you think you know. But, as it is, you sit with one hand in the pie and the other hand stuck in your mouth. How can you be fed? Your mouth is crammed full of your own ideology. Let me say this, swallow your food and empty your mouth. This is not the pie you want. Take your hand out of the pie you think contains the sweet taste of Love you seek. It appears to be a delicious treat, for just look at the crust and its perfect form. And yet, it contains a fruit that bitters the stomach and makes the Holy Child sick from its sour, unripened fruit. -Father-

"I am the Light of the world." Rev. Pam ACIM CC

Let Love Happen Today
"and so, it is" Rev. Reja ACIM OE CC 2015

When the multitude becomes One, the ascendance occurs. Stop trying to convince yourself it is so, and so it is. Receive the Peace. The Source within cannot be seen on the outside, until it is seen within. Let us go back to Song of Prayer the multitude is singing. The baritone and tenor are singing different notes and an apparently different song at one time. Be ye free of your despair. Lift your head high and sing the Song of Redemption: "Be ye restored". Life is indeed eternal. Let not your gifts single you out today. Sing the same song and different song at the same time. If you create competition, you create war. Be yourselves among your differences and you will find you are singing the same song indeed. -Father-

"You cannot tell a lie, without also telling the Truth at the same time." Derek Broes, The Global Witness, 2018

Standing Naked Before the World
"My true identity abides in You." Rev. Pam ACIM CC Lesson 283

Revelation is given you today. What has stood behind you, stands before you in the timeless. The dark, egoic thoughts of "past" experience are pulled to the forefront, acknowledged and released into the aqueous. -Father-

It is in letting go of illusions of Love we find ourselves unclothed before the world. We are letting go of that which we thought protected us from the savagery of the ego's premise of the worthless identity. At first, it feels like a vulnerable stance, but this too is an illusion dear child. The Holy Son of God is not a fragile creation. Our Father does not make the weak and desolate. His strength is beyond your fragile imagining. He is the Eternal and so are you because you contain Him. Look at the message in the dream. Is this a message of hope and strength? No, it is a message of destruction. In the end, you found yourself alone and afraid because your "source" of Love and support was gone.

Your brother's final message to you became your identity and you fully believed in his version of your reality. Where is the Love, and respect for yourself my, dear Child? We are One and Love is Real. How is it you think you find Love in the loveless concepts of the ego's world. Look within for the Answer.

"There it is," sweetheart: Love. It is not wrong to want to be Loved and respected dear One. Do not choose for disaster by not listening to your heart. What has been your brother's message to you? That you are unworthy of both respect and Love? How can this be True? The very concept of being unworthy of Love is a lie dear Child. You are Love. How can you be unworthy of what you are? If your brother finds you unworthy of his Love, he must find himself also unworthy. Is the dream wrong or is the "source" the problem here? Let us look at your dreams of Love. What is missing here? Your fantasy of your brother and the reality are quite stark. Why is this so? He simply does not Love himself and finds himself guilty over and over in his acts of unquitted love with several instead of the One within.

You cannot find Love where it does not exist. Do not worship your brother, for he has no idea what he is doing. You have made him your idol and find yourself empty and bereft. Look to me for the Answer. I know you are frightened, for you have believed more in your brother's version of reality than mine. Fantasy of your brother is in your mind, not his. He is to busy hiding from himself to pay attention to your fantasies of his love for you. Whoops, you placed your identity outside of yourself again. Let us repair this lack of belief in what you contain as a Child of the Most High. - Father -

"The Truth needs no defense." Lee ACIM OE CC

The Return to Innocence
"Let go of the fear ... Let it be soon ..." Jesus 2017

Drop the defensive character child, for it is not necessary. God is goodness and mercy, embodied in the goodness of Love. Let go of the fear of your innocence. Let go of the defensive character for just a moment. Let yourself take in, with each inward breath that Love quite simply Is. Exhale the notion, for a moment, that you need to protect yourself. Think for a moment, on your next in breath, of a cherished, lovely memory. Drop the defensive character on your next out breath and inhale deeply the Love in this cherished moment. I cannot stress enough the importance of allowing the moments of release into Love's presence each day.

Allow yourself to be a child again and look innocently at the world around you, now not having to pretend that you now know what anything is for. Dear child, feel the simple entrance of innocence when Love enters once again. You can feel the deep rush of Love within but be prepared to weep when innocent Love looks you in the eyes and smiles at your own innocence in return. Go within and find your cherished, loving memories soon. I would dare say there are those among you who might say this is child's play. I say to you, maybe it is in the child's play we will find the innocent Love once again. - Father-

"Don't place God in a box." Rhett ACIM OE CC 2018

The Purpose of the Time Share
"Who unblessed the bread?" Wendy ACIM OE CC 2018

It is in the grace of God, we stand before time and see its true use. It is important to remember who is doing what here in this moment. God's grace lies within the mind formed at the conception of Life. Is it not folly to believe, you and your cherished pieces of property are but, dust in an ever-shifting wind you call time, in a vacuum you call space, dear Brother? Which thinking is skewed here in this moment? I keep finding you are rather constantly dreaming of things gone by, or to come, without any true reference point that starts in the "now". As the mind floats along its perceived concepts of time in a linear fashion, the mind and thought systems get stuck in the ruts of past, present and future concepts.

But, indeed, how does one place linear spokes on an infinite concept, such as Love, and its eternal moment that beats in every vibratory aspect of Creation? This is the problem with the idea that a moment in time can ever cease to be so. What follows the moment ceases? Well, it seems to go to a place called your memory.

It seems then, memory must exist outside the timeline, where moments cease to be and fall back on the eternal concept of Love. So, what is this idea that we trade with each other pieces of our time share, before this moment ceases to be on the timeline and its consequent death ideology? How can something, and I mean anything, cease to exist and still exist at the same time. unless it is eternal? This is the absurdity of the ego and why as we all fell asleep, we were all laughing. When we awaken, we will laugh once again. -Father-

"The Kingdom of Heaven is spread over the Earth but many do not see it." Gospel of Thomas, The Secret Teachings of Jesus

... Stay in the Good, and Pray ...

CHAPTER FOUR

The Tomb

All is found forgiven in the tomb. The harsh judgements are traded for loving caress. It is the womb of regeneration. A time to heal and understand what you chose and why. It is moments of healing laughter, mixed with music and Joy. The tomb fills with the Living Light and the luminous water are offered up. -Father-

The Shroud of Jesus
"Let it go ... flowing down and out." Sied ACIM OE CC 2015

Accept the release to Joy. Do not fear your tears. The brave face to the masses becomes the weeping man behind the woodshed. Become cleansed by your tears. Heal the wounds perceived by the Holy Mind.

"Release it ... let it go ... flowing down and out." As the vessel empties, it can be filled to overflowing with the living, luminous waters. The Holy Oneness is restored to the Sonship. Accept the gifts of God and decline your heritage no more. You are the limitless, most, Holy Child of the Living God. -Father-

"God is in His Holy Temple." Rev. Pam ACIM CC

Suits in the Closet
"You do not have to say the word "death". Your Son is not there, but he is not dead." Fran ACIM OE CC 2018

The entrance to heaven is not at death's doorstep. Heaven is a state of Love. Those who cannot tolerate Love, cannot tolerate heaven. Your ego is pointing you in the wrong direction through its lie that heaven's return lies at its doorstep called death. What a lonely concept it is, that one must leave all you Love to find heaven. That, indeed, Love is torn apart and can no longer exist except in our memories in bodies. The ego believes and convinces you that Love only exists while in form. I ask you a simple question here: who is it that remains in your memory once we hang our skins in the closet of suits called death?

Who is it that animated the suits now hanging in the graveyard of finality you have created for yourselves? What if I told you, you have clearly been lied to and believed the lie that relationship ceases outside of the body. Look within dear Brother and you will find you have continued to have relationship with every "departed" Loved One. Why is this so? Because, indeed, there is no departure. Only you have believed this to be so, and so it is. Take off your brother's suit and see He who stands before you and whom you Love dearly. They are here but awaiting your recognition. -Father-

Let us focus on the Living concepts of God, living within our Loving relationships with one another. God does not live in dismay, discord and death. God does not live after death, but before it and before it was ever conceived of in the minds of His children.
-Father-

"Life is about knowing which question to ask." Al Sanchez, 2017

Let it Be Soon
"You cannot maintain the illusion of loneliness if you are not alone." Lee ACIM OE CC Ch 8: Section 5: #26

Our Father within, does not look upon the finite with any concern for its effects upon His created order of things. What man has created for himself is, but a temporary ideology of what has never been so. It is not up to man to decide the order of creation or its laws. For, this was decided for long before time's conception in the minds of His children.

Our Father is a Good and Loving God. He has no need for the sacrifices His Son attempts to lay at His feet. His lonely child is called Home to the remembrance of His Father's Love, residing within his heart. Love has no need for sacrifice. For, it is nothing.

The Holy Child is looking for his Home where it cannot be found. And, in his search, the Child thinks the laws of this world are the laws of his Father. So, he brings loss, despair and separation to the altar thinking these sacrificial concepts will gain access to divine salvation and entrance to a place called heaven. Clearly, the Holy Child does not understand who he is and from wence he comes.

He has forgotten his true Home and the Love that rules and creates the universe he sees before him. Sacrifice will not bring the Holy Child Home, but Love will. Sacrifice of any kind is not warranted. The Son of God does have to tear and break off pieces of himself to gain heaven. -Father-

Our Daily Bread

Our Father, Who Art within. Give us this day our daily
bread, that we may look upon each other with Love
which can only come from sharing with each other,
the bread of Life within. The living witness of God
cannot be found in separate concepts of Love. To receive Love is a blessed experience. And to give Love
is the same blessing in return.
-Father-

Welcome the Coming of the Guest
"Where judgement was, I look upon the Light." Rev. Pam ACIM CC

I call upon the name of Our Father within to bestow upon
Us the corrective sight. Whatever stands unforgiven in you,
stands in judgement of your brother. What remains in bitterness is the sweet taste of sorrow upon your tongue. Is it not
strange to you, you love your sorrow? I say to you, it is within,
you will find release from your guilt and grief. For, you hold to
tightly to your dreams of sorrow, in a past you remember all
too well, yet faintly, in a place you call time. Most of what you
hold against each other, exists there. Each, having a different
version of a piece in the timeline, seen from different perspec-
tives with different projected content. And yet, there are no
true differences. -Father-

The Guest
Our Father Who Art the Light of Heaven within,
blessed be Thy Holy Name. For Your Holy Light re-
stores our sight, and reminds us of Our Eternal Identity in You.
Your temple lies within Our Hearts, but awaiting recognition. There is no identity outside of You, Father,

we want.

We will seek and find your Loving breath, replenishing Our Hearts with the Love which has always been so.

Your children are beckoning to You, Our Father, to bring Us Home to Ourselves, and Our True Identity within Our hearts.

We pray for, and accept, the Holy Instant, and the release from the bondage of our ego, only true Revelation can bring.

Let us not deny our true identity, living within Our hearts. Release us from our judgements, and let us be pure in heart.

For the harsh judgements we place upon ourselves, we place upon our brothers and cannot find the Truth of Love we need to remember.

Blessed be the name of Our Father, who is Love and Truth embodied within Us All, each blessed moment. - Father -

Hide and Seek

"I merely follow, for I would not lead." Rev. Pam ACIM CC Lesson 324

You see dear, Holy Child, the ego plays a vicious game of hide and seek with you. It is not in its best interest to be found. For, once it is found it cannot hide again. Its ploy against your sanity are basically the same at the larger and smaller scales. The ego uses fear to keep you apart and alienated from Love. Do not be blind to yourself and place your allegiance in finite concepts of who among you is most wisely using the ego's format; of who is right and who is wrong. Killing is killing, no matter which side of the fence you have placed yourself on. Hate is what is always being chosen for when death and killing are the outcome. Would humanity truly ever choose for mass extinction? Is this not why, they try to bring God into their concepts of war and death, and use eternal gifts as their just reward for their sacrifice? - Father –

"Miracles are a way of undoing over-learned patterns of lack of Love." Helen Schuckman

Within the Parentheses
"If I am thinking a bad thought, I need to stay out of it like a bad neighborhood." Carla ACIM OE CC 2017

The stumbling blocks you are experiencing are inherent in the process of learning. The ego is truly afraid of self-discovery. The eternal self lies at the core of the unmasking process. As the masks of the defensive character are peeled away, the true, loving character of the Soul begins to shine through. The defensive character is set up at the out-set of the separation experience. - Father -

When the umbilicus is severed, so then, is the Holy Child cut off consciously from his life Source. The severing of the cord in correspondence represents the loss of the conscious awareness of the Eternal Source of Life. The new born babe must find a new source of oxygen for its blood and a new source of food for its energy. The mother can no longer provide these directly into the blood of life. The separation experience is generally painful at its outset. The egoic version of Life is up-ended and full of mishap. - Father -

It is a seemingly, endless search that eventually leads the child to his own naval in search of Peace. The child eventually runs to back to the beginning to find, what lay at the last breath was also there before the first breath. Life in a body, is like a word contained in parenthesis within a sentence of total meaning. You cannot glean any information from the word contained in the parenthesis. For, it is outside of the contained word, the true meaning of the sentence is found. Such is the true meaning of the sentence of Life. - Father -

You are having a parenthetical experience of a much greater Truth.

Anna is (Love)
The Holy Child is (Love)

And, Love cannot be contained for long, for it is not Love's nature. Freedom is part of Love's nature. It is effervescent like unto to fragrance of the Lily. Do you not understand, you exist within creation right now in this moment? The stillness surrounds you if you "let all thing be as they are". God is in each moment if you invite Him in. You cannot stand on both sides. - Father –

"I am not alone, and I would not intrude my past upon my guest. I have invited him, and he is here." Lee ACIM OE CC

Expect Miracles
"My judgements have hurt me." Lee ACIM OE CC 2018

Forgiveness of your brother is forgiveness of yourself, for in him is your memory restored that to give and receive are one in Truth. Be ye the provider of the miracle of the Love you contain. For, it is not a fantasy, your brother needs you and you need him. Through your sacred remembrance, you remember heaven together. Once again, let go of the contained matter of the illusion. Be honest with yourselves. Can you not yet see, the gathering up and collecting of forms of matter is indeed meaningless? How can something without life be useful to you? Indeed, it is in the meaning you ascribe to it, which gives it any meaning at all. Listen to the voice of reason you contain. All is within you.

All meaning comes from within. Therefore, it is a fallacy to let others ascribe meaning for you. This is also why, the Course you are studying is changing your mind and thought structure. Understanding the division that occurred and the answer you contain within to heal this division, is critical to the waking process. Your mind is being stirred into the remembrance of the Eternal Holy Mind you contain. As your memory returns, you will be less engaged with the clumps of matter and more concerned with the Life Source they contain and the true content of Life. - Father-

"Prayer is the medium of miracles. Prayer is the natural communication between the created and the Creator. Through prayer love is received, and through miracles love is expressed." ACIM OE Ch 1:11

What is there to gain in withholding the words you contain? Once again, I return you to the forgiveness of the self, you seek to judge. Ask, and ye shall receive the return to the awareness of all you contain. Do not let your brother dampen your spirits and lead you into dismay. "Lead him in the way of the One you follow." It is not up to you to unravel his illusions for him, but to unravel your own illusions of him. Let go of the idea, you know the way out, for this is why you follow my lead through the Holy Spirit residing in your heart. I cannot help those who are not yet willing to help themselves. Look upon all things with innocence, for innocence is not fragile as you have been taught. - Father –

"I need do nothing, but not interfere." Lee ACIM OE CC Ch 16:1:4

The Forgiven One
"I will there be Light." Rev. Pam ACIM CC

For, we have all fallen and fallen short of the grace of God, but in His mercy, He finds us perfect still. Who is it to say the man cub will see the folly of the erroneous belief system he, himself has no understanding of whence it comes? Following along these guidelines, he finds himself lost and beating his war drum of fear. – Father –

"Forgiveness is my function as the Light of the world." Aida ACIM OE CC 2018

Every interaction is the answer to a question in a future interaction. When given to the Holy Spirit's care, through forgiveness, all things become whole once again. The choice for death is a choice for despair. Why, dear child would you choose for this to be the outcome? - Father -

"I rest in God." Rev. Pam ACIM Lesson 109

Giving and Receiving
"The unloving behaviors of others are the fear they are project-ing onto me." Chris ACIM OE CC 2018

What is Love without extension? Indeed, Revelation without extension is meaningless. In order to give, you must have received, thus making the two indistinguishable. You must have received Love in order to give Love. Imagine, if you will, never being able to Love one another through the extension of the Revelation of Love? Thus, the saying, "it is more blessed to give than to receive". - Father –

"Without forgiveness will your dreams remain to terrify you." Rev. Pam ACIM CC Review Part 2

Sit and ride behind me, beside me and before me and be my

voice. It is through our joining of heart with mind, we find each other. You, my dear keep leaving yourself out of the conversation, as if your words, your thoughts and your part in this process are irrelevant. Let us look at this before we continue. It is time for an open discussion.

You are the Love you seek. The empty abyss of the ego can never be filled, for it seeks for Love from the wrong source. The only one you hide from is yourself. You run into your cave and hide from all concepts of Love and extension, hoping Love will come to you. But, dear One, this very concept is contrary to the laws of creation. To give and receive are one. So, you hide in your cave awaiting rescue. Are you waiting for someone to find you in your silence? Look into my eyes and see the innocent, eternal Soul you contain. You are seeking for Love in loveless concepts. The ego structure exists in the complete inversion of Truth. The weak, the timid, the powerless are all results of the ego's displacement of source. – Father –

"We are living in the wrong story." Laurie ACIM OE CC 2018

The Resurrection
"The ultimate purpose of all learning is to abolish fear." Rev. Pam ACIM CC

Be joyful for death has been transcended and understood. Wholeness is restored in the mind and the split mind is healed. Two worlds have become one and the nightmares are finally over. True usefulness is now possible, the blocks to Love are gone. Fear is gone, only Love remains. -Father-

"Be ye observer". Gospel of Thomas, The Secret Teachings of Jesus

This is the first lifting of the awareness that meaning does not lie outside of the mind. It is your interpretation of all things which gives them any meaning at all. The placement of meaning outside of the mind is the relinquishment of your power to the illusory content of the dream. I must bring you to the awareness that you contain the power to change the content and see the Love beyond the veil the ego has placed before your eyes. The power lies with the dreamer, not in the dreams of various forms of thought. - Father -

Project Love, see Love. Project hate, see hate. So, we start with the simple content of the dream. We later progress to the complex mind content, such as our relationships. If you are projecting emotional context on the material contained in the world, how much more are you doing this in relationship with your brothers. So, thus, we come back to the content of the mind: Love or fear being the movers of meaning. Release yourself and let me show you the way out. – Father –

Do not look behind you for what lies before you, for then you seek to make them the same. Let this moment be given to you and then your past, present and future will not be the same. What lies before you still remains unseen. At this point in your development, you will see in shifts of insight and Revelation. The inner visions of Truth will become more consistent in your awareness. – Father –

"Be a companion to those who are willing to leave hell behind."
Mari Perron, A Course of Love, 2017

Love is always the answer. Offer forgiveness to your brother for his past transgressions against you. But, be careful of being the victor's fool. In your brother's unawareness of his ego, he will bring the same transgression against you time and time again. It is your awareness of the game being played by the ego that brings it to a halt, through the new boundaries you place before him. Expecting your brother to change, is indeed ludicrous, because he is not aware of his existence within a divided mind. The mind state of most men exists outside of their own understanding. This is not to say, he is bereft of all understanding. Give to him a gentle touch, but a firm boundary set in Truth and emanating from the Love in your heart. – Father -

"It is the Love that is important here." Rev. Pam ACIM CC

Correction from the harsh rod of the ego offers your brother attack, not hope. Control and Love are very different starting points for correction. If you look at your brother's back you will see the lash marks of previous attack. What is there to gain in adding more? In Truth, the more lashes you add the stronger the ego becomes in both of you. How is this the answer to healing? Joining is an aspect of Love, separation belongs to the ego. If you are reacting, you are not leading your brother, but following in his footsteps. Now, you are both lost in concepts of attack, adding more lash marks to your hearts and minds. Look to me and find true brotherhood, for I know the way out of your sorrow and in to the Light of true understanding of each other. Look to your hearts before you speak. – Father –

"I do not understand anything I see in this room [on this street, from this window, in this place]" Rev. Pam ACIM CC Lesson 3

The illusion, meaning lies outside yourself, is the concept in the mind being challenged here. Lift the adjectives and only see the neutral form of the object. This brings us back to the essence of being. It shows us the starting and ending point of all the lessons contained within the Holy Child. It reminds you what lies at the core of your existence and why you exist at all. "God is but Love, and therefore so am I." You are because Love Is. The child thinks the words give the understanding, but the words are the initial steps, releasing the mind into the unknown. The mind has not yet understood, it was conceived from Love. – Father –

The Holy Child contains the answer because Our Father does not exist separate from His creations. It is not a fallacy to believe, what man has made has more inherent value than what Our Father has created. Identity cannot be found in idols that decay and turn to dust. – Father –

"And now, we see with the eyes of the heart." Mari Perron, A Course of Love, 2017

Allow only Loving content into your mind. Close the door to the past you no longer want to occupy your mind and make real. The present moment is bereft of your conscious awareness, because the shadow figures in your mind are leading you where you will to take them: around blind corners and down endless, dark corridors. – Father –

Everyone brings lessons to the table. Do not separate yourself from humanity. Our Father does not see separation among His children, for they are one, beautiful, conscious awareness of Love. Creation was placed before man to remember the majesty of Our Father within. You are One with His creation. You do not exist outside of it. The mind of man is in a slumber. Indeed, some believe creation to be "dead" without intelligence or meaning, so they ruthlessly destroy the environment around them, thinking there is no recourse for their actions. Man does not need to fix creation. He needs to understand, science without Source clearly intact and understood creates endless theories without resolution. – Father -

The Masters have come to teach those who will listen the true, creative principles and Divine Laws of Our Father. Mankind, should lend an ear to their teachings, exit theory and enter the Truth that all comes from Love. The miracle comes in your darkest hours, when the barricades to Love have become so great, you cannot traverse the wall you have placed before yourself. Your ego has convinced you, you are alone. You can walk through this wall, once you know you can. – Father–

You can always be in a transcendent place within no matter what is placed in or around you. I am always here. You, but need call on my name in recognition of this Truth. We are One in Our Father. We are entitled to His eternal blessings. – Father –

"I can elect to change all thoughts that hurt." Rev. Pam ACIM CC Lesson 284

You have the Right to Remain in the Silence
"Ma, why are you hiding" Joseph Andrew Billings 2018

You see dear Child, you and I have something in common, for I to was released from the Himalayan mountains, still an innocent child, to walk the valley of the shadows amongst men who despised themselves and each other. I lived in the illusions of their dark hatred and maintained my innocence through my silence. Indeed child, silence is golden when put to Love's use. – Father -

"wait ... for it ..." Al Sanchez, 2018

Fowl Language
"Our strength is in our Joy Rev. Pam ACIM CC

AM: I was sitting in the living room in my big comfy chair and went within to spend time with Father. HM: Can birds control their bowels.

AM: What? ...

HM: I would venture to say no, or ... they just don't give a shit.

AM: I started laughing at his absurd sense of humor. I had been feeling so serious. So, consumed with me. He always has a way of making me laugh. I got onto him for his use of "fowl" language. We laughed together for quite some time.

HM: I have a question for the group this morning: "How is making your brother your enemy helpful to you?"

The Imagined World

"I have given what I see in this room {on this street, from this window, in this place}, all the meaning it has for me." Rev. Pam ACIM CC Lesson 2

You must do for your brother what has been done for you. You cannot control the narrative and hope for healing. There is nothing you need do, but be willing to receive the blessing of the Holy Spirit's Peace in all situations. You will not find Peace in the outer world you see, for it is born of the chaos within the egoic thought system. The constructs of this system of thought are self-destructive. So, how can Peace be found? Do not be fooled into thinking you can conquer something you do not yet understand. – Father –

"The body is a fence the Son of God imagines he has built to separate parts of his Self from other parts." Rev. Pam ACIM CC Lesson 270

The Ascension

"There is nothing to forgive, except my own perception." Sondra ACIM OE CC 2018

This is the final understanding, there is no real level change. It is the opening of the portal within, the continuous flow across the bridge. One mind restored: the flow restored. Existence is understood as loving and truly useful; a gentle hand extending Love, kind words and blessings. -Father-

There are no shadows within the Light. All darkness disolves in Love's presence. Do not be dismayed by fearful content, for it is nothing. Call it nothing and so it is. Do not the content of dark illusions the ego displays before you. Its purpose is distraction, for you are getting closer to your final release of its grip on your heart and mind. Forgive it even though you do not understand it and its true meaning will become clear to you. I cannot take this step for you as you must look upon your fear and choose for the Holy Spirit's loving answer. The Holy Instant arrives at your request. Your release is always sure. Fear is an obstacle overcome through Love and forgiveness of your brother and yourself for what was never true. - Father -

"Unbind Jesus." Rhett ACIM OE CC 2018

The Holy Womb
"The world is full of miracles who stand in shining silence." Lee ACIM OE CC

It is with great Joy, I share this Holy news with you. It is time mankind put an end to karmic retribution once and for all! The ego, thought system has complicated your understanding, ensuring you never figure out the final move, and its demise. The Queen, Our, Holy Mother holds the Love of Our Father's creation in Her, Holy womb of time, child. Her deep Love cannot be circumvented. She sees the whole court and can act in all directions, inner-dimensionally. She sees the All of Creation lying at Her, Holy Feet. She Loves and protects the Christ within in us all, residing within the sanctuary of Her Holy Womb. The crossover of karma from lifetime to lifetime, is a cycle of retribution. – Father –

"Father, we lost our way for a while." Rev. Pam ACIM CC Lesson 293

The Forgiven One
"Everything is eternal, and everything is internal." Derek Broes, The Global Witness, 2018

If, I forgive myself for my errors and you forgive yourself for your errors, then we forgive each other and walk surely forward in this moment, what then is left? We have no need of the war drum of fear.
- Father -

"Where darkness was, I look upon Light." Rev. Pam ACIM CC Lesson 302

AM: Night after night, I have been having nightmares. Why? What are they for? It feels like I am being purged of all kinds of darkness I have held onto across lifetimes. It is exhausting!

Vision: Jesus and I are standing right in front of lucifer and his legions. Lucifer made a threatening stance and dark wings fluttered in the darkness. Then Jesus spoke to lucifer: "You are nothing, for you were created from nothing, return thus." Lucifer and his legions vanished. Your nightmares are nothing and this is th lesson. Fearful content is created from what is truly impossible. What you have held onto must be released through its acknowledgement. Yes, it is exhausting to look at, yet it is even more exhausting to hold onto. Do not depair, it will end in Joy and laughter as you learn to play again and no longer living in darkened dreams of hopeless despair. Forgive it all. Every dark dream will be vanquished in the Light of forgiveness. You will have
no more reasons to hold onto its vacant illusions of your true

reality. - Father -

God is within His Holy Temple within your heart of Love. His Light knows of no darkness and looks upon it as a stranger to Love and His Son and Loves it away. The answer is the same to all situations the Son of God may find himself in. The entrance of Love is the vanquishment of all darkness. Learn to Love again and your freedom from all nightmares is sure. I Love You in name of the Holy One within your heart. We are of One mind created from One Love and nothing else is sure, nor above this Truth. The Holy Child is cherished and nourished through the Holy breath of Our Mother. Remember, this answer when fear has entered and be free of it forever more. - Father -

Breath goodness into your existence. Breath in ... breathe out ... and let go of what was never so. With focus the breath becomes deeper as you let go of all the hesitation toward Love's entry. Conflicting wills cannot be my will. - Father -

Dust in the Wind
"And, nothing conflicts with the holy Truth that I remain as you created me." Rev. Pam ACIM CC

The eternal moment, contains the Love you have been seeking dear, Holy Child. Forgiveness, brings the Holy Instant and the Revelation, releasing the remembrance of what you have always contained within. You are Love. It created you. How can you not contain it? But your egos have convinced you, it lies somewhere out there under the rainbow of illusions. You cannot find me unless you look for me within, under the coat of many colors.

The illusion that sacrifice facilitates this healing blessing is indeed ludicrous, for sacrifice exist in externals. Our Father and the Christ lie within, so how can external sacrifice have any true meaning. Let go of the external world, for it seems great indeed as it looks so big and important before your eyes. But dear child, it contains nothing you truly need, as you have more than all of this "dust in the wind" within you. You are an eternal creation. The finite offers you nothing. Let it go! Let it all go and find the Truth, my Love. – Father -

And now, we will pretend and come to understand that the ego does not exist. It never did and never will in Truth, for it is nothing. You do not have to grasp, nor understand its premise, for it has none. It seeks from the unknown the known to try and know itself. Does this impossible scenerio seem reasonable to you? Let us start from the known and work our way from there. What is known? Pick up the dust beneath your feet and feel what the trinkets and gadgets of ego become. It is all dust in the wind, my friend. So what remains, but the memories of Love's refrain. The cries of your newborn fill you with laughter as you feel God's gift of song in your newborn's need for his mother's milk is sung.
- Father -

Look upon the Holy World with the kind eyes of a child. There is no need to wait on the Master. For, He always comes when the night is cold. His Light exudes warmth filling the cold, inner spaces of your heart with the heat of Love. Do not believe, the night and seeming, eternal darkness will consume you. For, I have come at last. You will awaken with the dawn, and I will not leave your mind again. As your eyes open, you will find, my Light does not hurt them. Gentle sounds will meet your ears and Joy will fill your heart. So, do not be afraid of the come what may. -Father-

"Nothing I see in this room [on this street, from this window, in this place] means anything." ACIM OE Lesson 1

"In a three,

in a two,

in a,

Oneness ..."

Rev. Pamela Whitman ACIM CC

"Nothing real can be threatened,
nothing unreal exists. Herein, lies the
peace of God" ACIM OE Intro

... Stay in the Good

and Pray ...

"The Chalice of Redemption is offered up to the child who believes he is, but a fleeting thought of God. But, God has no fleeting
thoughts. All of His creation proceeds from clear intention." The
World Within

NOTES

Special Soup or Hippocrates Soup

1 medium celery root, if available (if not, 3 to 4 celery branches)
1 medium parsley root (rarely available; may be omitted)
2 small or 1 large leek (if not available; 2 small onions) 2 medium onions
Garlic to taste
Small amount of parsley
1 ½ pounds if tomatoes (or more if desired)
1 pound of potatoes

Wash and scrub vegetables and cut into slices or ½ inch cubes. Put in large pot, add water to just cover vegetables, bring to a boil, then cook slowly on low heat for 1 1/2 hours until all the vegetables are soft. Pass through a food mill to remove fibers. Let soup cool before storing in the refrigerator.

REFERENCES

A Cancer Therapy, Results of Fifty Cases and The Cure of Advanced Cancer by Diet Therapy: A Summary of Thirty Years of Clinical Experimentation, Max Gerson, MD, Gerson Institute, San Diego, CA, 2002

A Course of Love, Combined Volume, Mari Peron, Take Heart Publications, Nevada City, California, 2014

A Course in Miracles, Helen Schucman, Course in Miracles Society, Poc Org edition, 2009 Divine Love and Wisdom, Emmanuel Swedenborg, Swedenborg Foundation, West Chester, Pennsylvania, 2003

Healing the Gerson Way, Defeating Cancer and Other Chronic Diseases, Charlotte Gerson with Beata Bishop, Gerson Health Media, Carmel, California, 2007

Life and Teachings of the Masters of the Far East, Volume 1 and Volume 2, Baird T. Spalding, DeVorss Publications, Camarillo, California, 1927

The Secret Teachings of Jesus, Four Gnostic Gospels, Marwin W. Meyer, First Vintage Books Edition, A Division of Random House, New York, 1986.

The Teachings of the Inner Ramana, Regina Dawn Akers, Diamond

Anna Billings-Vice

Clear Vision, 2005

The Woman's Study Bible, The New King James Version, Thomas Nelson Publishers, Nashville, Tennessee,

Your Immortal Reality, How to Break the Cycle of Birth and Death, Gary Renard, Hay House, Carlsbad, California, 2006

Made in the USA
Middletown, DE
14 March 2020